Margaret Strong, Toy Collector

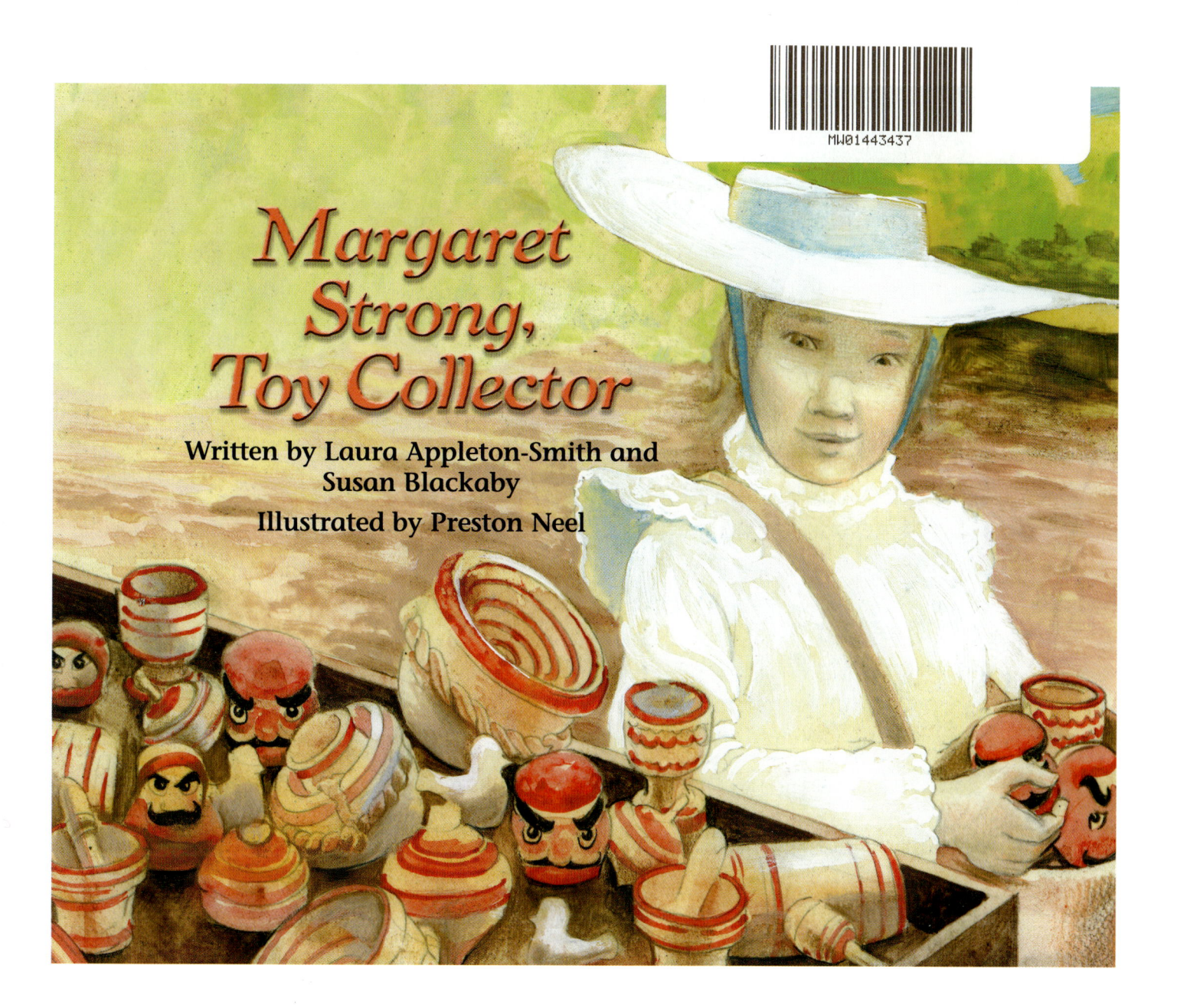

Written by Laura Appleton-Smith and Susan Blackaby

Illustrated by Preston Neel

Laura Appleton-Smith was born and raised in Vermont and holds a degree in English from Middlebury College. Laura is a primary school teacher who has combined her talents in creative writing and her experience in early childhood education to create *Books to Remember*. Laura lives in New Hampshire with her husband, Terry.

Susan Blackaby has worked in educational publishing for over 30 years. In addition to her writing curriculum, she is the author of *Rembrandt's Hat* (Houghton Mifflin, 2002); *Cleopatra: Egypt's Last and Greatest Queen* (Sterling, 2009); *Nest, Nook, and Cranny* (Charlesbridge, 2010), winner of the 2011 Lion and the Unicorn Award for Excellence in North American Poetry; and *Brownie Groundhog and the February Fox* (Sterling, 2011). She lives in Portland, Oregon.

Preston Neel was born in Macon, Georgia. Greatly inspired by Dr. Seuss, he decided to become an artist at the age of four. Preston's advanced art studies took place at the Academy of Art College San Francisco. Now Preston pursues his career in art with the hope of being an inspiration himself, particularly to children who want to explore their endless bounds. Illustrations have been created based on images provided courtesy of The Strong®.

Text copyright © 2012 Laura Appleton-Smith and Susan Blackaby
Illustration copyright © 2012 Preston Neel

All Rights Reserved
No part of this book may be reproduced or transmitted in any form or by any means, electronic, mechanical, photocopying, recording, or otherwise, without prior written permission from the publisher.
For information, contact Flyleaf Publishing.

A Book to Remember™
Published by Flyleaf Publishing

For orders or information, contact us at **(800) 449-7006**.
Please visit our website at **www.flyleafpublishing.com**

Eighth Edition 2/20
Library of Congress Catalog Card Number: 2013930432
ISBN-13: 978-1-60541-152-1
Printed and bound in the USA at Worzalla Publishing, Stevens Point, WI

*The Strong is a highly interactive, collections-based
educational institution devoted to the study and exploration of play.
Collections include hundreds of thousands of historical objects related to play,
including the world's largest and most comprehensive collection of dolls, toys, and games.
Many thanks to The Strong for helping us to tell Margaret Strong's story.*

LAS

To the Red-Tailed Readers.

SB

To all the toy makers in the world.

PN

Photographs courtesy of The Strong®, Rochester, New York 2012

Do you have a big box of shells or a bag of marbles?

Do you have a stack of comics that you keep
in a safe spot?

Do you keep or trade baseball cards?

2

People who enjoy marbles, comics, pens, or stamps tend to have more than just one of these things.

People who have a lot of one thing are called *collectors*.

4

Lots of people collect things. They find an object they like, then they find another and another and another!

Collecting things can be a fun hobby. For Margaret Strong, collecting toys was a fun hobby and a lifelong job.

6

Margaret Strong was born in 1897.

When Margaret was a little girl,
her mom collected artifacts from Japan.
Her dad liked to collect coins.

8

In 1907, Margaret joined her parents
on a seven-month trip around the world.
While other girls and boys were sitting in class,
Margaret was visiting all different points on the globe.

She rode elephants in India.
She went to museums in Japan.
She ate oysters in Hong Kong.

10

To pass the time on these trips, Margaret started to collect toys.

On each trip, Margaret had a bag with her. Her mom and dad told her that she could get any toy she wanted as long as it fit into her bag.

12

At first, Margaret had a hard time making choices.
Her day of shopping would end very quickly
if she filled up her bag with one big toy.

Then Margaret got smart....
She discovered that if she avoided big toys,
she could fill her bag with lots of small toys.
Margaret had turned into a collector!

14

Time passed. Margaret had a family of her own.
She had a big house, and it was filled with toys.

She collected pull toys and games.
She collected blocks and puzzles.

16

Margaret collected doll houses, and dolls, too.
Margaret collected over 27,000 dolls!

In fact, Margaret Strong collected so many toys in
her lifetime that now there is a museum named after her!

18

If you are interested, you can see
many of Margaret Strong's toys on display
at a museum called The Strong.

The Strong is in Rochester, New York.
It is the biggest toy museum in the world.

20

Think about the things you enjoy collecting.
Can you think of having so much of that thing that you could fill your house?

Could your hobby fill a museum?
Keep collecting and find out!

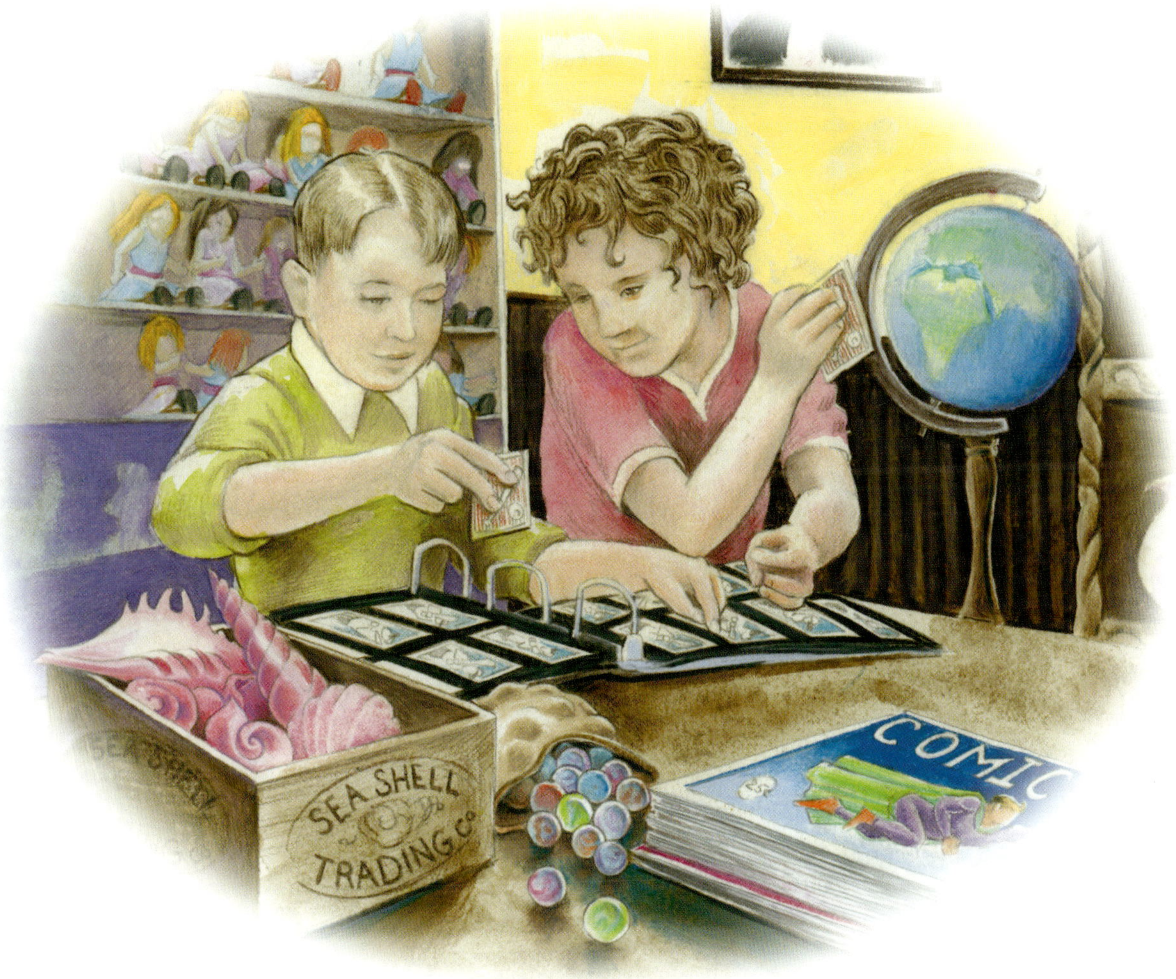
SEA SHELL TRADING Co.
COMIC

Prerequisite Skills
Single consonants and short vowels
Final double consonants **ff**, **gg**, **ll**, **nn**, **ss**, **tt**, **zz**
Consonant /k/ **ck**
Consonant /j/ **g**, **dge**
Consonant /s/ **c**
/ng/ **n[k]**
Consonant digraphs /ng/ **ng**, /th/ **th**, /hw/ **wh**
Consonant digraphs /ch/ **ch**, **tch**, /sh/ **sh**, /f/ **ph**
Schwa /ə/ **a**, **e**, **i**, **o**, **u**
Long /ā/ **a_e**
Long /ē/ **e_e**, **ee**, **y**
Long /ī/ **i_e**, **igh**
Long /ō/ **o_e**
Long /ū/, /o͞o/ **u_e**
r-Controlled /ar/ **ar**
r-Controlled /or/ **or**
r-Controlled /ûr/ **er**, **ir**, **ur**, **ear**, **or**, **[w]or**
/ô/ **al**, **all**
/ul/ **le**
/d/ or /t/ **–ed**

Target Letter-Sound Correspondence

/oi/ sound spelled **oi**

avoided	joined
choices	points
coins	

Target Letter-Sound Correspondence

/oi/ sound spelled **oy**

boys	toy
enjoy	toys
oysters	

High-Frequency Puzzle Words

about	of
another	one
any	other
are	out
around	over
be	own
could	people
day	pull
do	she
each	so
find	there
from	they
have	to
having	too
house	wanted
houses	was
into	were
many	who
more	would
new	you
now	your

Story Puzzle Words

discovered	museum
display	museums
India	told
month	

Decodable Words

1897	cards	fun	lifelong	quickly	then
1907	class	games	lifetime	Rochester	these
27,000	collect	get	like	rode	thing
a	collected	girl	liked	safe	things
after	collecting	girls	little	see	think
all	collector	globe	long	seven	time
an	collectors	got	lot	shells	trade
and	comics	had	lots	shopping	trip
artifacts	dad	hard	making	sitting	trips
as	different	her	marbles	small	turned
at	doll	hobby	Margaret	smart	up
ate	dolls	Hong Kong	mom	spot	very
bag	elephants	if	much	stack	visiting
baseball	end	in	named	stamps	went
big	fact	interested	object	started	when
biggest	family	is	on	Strong	while
blocks	fill	it	or	Strong's	with
born	filled	Japan	pass	tend	world
box	first	job	passed	than	York
called	fit	just	pens	that	
can	for	keep	puzzles	the	